Contents

Meet the Bulldog

The Bulldog—a grand canine indeed—a nearly ancient breed that descends from a long line of tough dogs that were originally used for bull- and bear-baiting. He may have started with a tougher-than-nails background, but the Bulldog now not only is considered the national dog of England but also has become a beloved family pet around the world.

In order to understand the Bulldog and his background, you must know a bit about the history of

With a face like no other in dogdom, the Bulldog is certainly one of the more recognizable breeds worldwide.

the fighting dog. Bull-running began in England as early as the mid-1300s. This was a "sport" whereby the bull was turned out among a crowd of minstrels; if the bull, who had had his ears and tail cut off and his body smeared with soap,

Despite fighting-dog origins, today's Bulldog is a lover!

was able to make it from Tutbury to Derbyshire without anyone cutting off a piece of his skin, he was considered to be safe. If someone was able to cut off a piece of him, the bull was then brought to the bullring in Tutbury and the dogs were brought in to bait him. When all was done, the king could dispose of the bull as he pleased. In later years, the bull was given to the duke of the area, was fed and then was given to the poor for eating at holiday time. The inhumane and unpleasant practice of bull-running continued until 1778, when it was abolished.

The Bulldog has an impressive head, wide chest, stocky build and strong legs—a sturdy dog indeed!

Bull-running, not as common as bull-baiting, was practiced in only three English towns, whereas bull-baiting was common and popular throughout England. The sport of baiting animals, and that included bears, lions, monkeys and eventually dog against dog as well as dog against bull, was very popular not only among the wealthy but also among the common people, who had little in the way of enter-tainment. The average peasant could breed a tough

The French Bulldog derived from smaller members of the English Bulldog breed. Along with smaller size, the Frenchie's signature "bat ears" differ from the rose ears of its English cousin.

dog, send it into the ring with a bull and take bets on who would win—the bull or the dog. People found these matches to be entertaining, while allowing the peasants to make a bit of money.

Dogs at that time were not bred for their looks but were bred for toughness, tenacity and spirit. The Bulldog who could pin the bull in the least amount of time, regardless of any injury to himself, became a prize, particularly if he could repeat this feat time after time, fighting in spite of any injuries. This dog was then bred to an equally tough dog with the hope of raising dogs who were equally as ferocious, or even more so, in the ring.

By the early 1800s, a group of individuals realized that the fighting of animals for sport was a cruel and inhumane activity, and laws were passed that eventually outlawed this practice. In

1835, all dog-fighting was outlawed in England. The Bulldog experienced a decline in popularity as a result, as owners no longer

This group of people set about to preserve the Bulldog's desirable characteristics as well as breed out (eliminate) the dog's fighting

The American Bulldog is a much longer-legged dog than the English. There is controversy as to whether the American Bulldog is descended from the English or derived from old-time American working dogs.

felt that these dogs had a purpose.

By 1860, dog shows were being held in England and a small group of fanciers thought that the grand Bulldog of the past should not fall into further decline.

instincts and other disagreeable habits. In 1875, a standard was drawn up by these exhibitors, stating just what the Bulldog should look like and act like, and this gave the breed the start that it needed on its road to preservation and, eventually, to popularity.

The two dogs who are considered to be the foundation of the modern Bulldog are Crib and Rosa. Illustrated in a painting dated 1817, the dogs have long tails, are much higher on leg than the present Bulldog and do not have the "pushed-in" face for which the Bulldog is so well known. Within time, the Pug was interbred with

Bulldogs seen in the show ring today are judged by a similar standard to those of yesteryear, drawn up by the pioneers in the breed.

the Bulldog, bringing down the height of the Bulldog and creating the shortened muzzle. A larger dog, named Toro, was imported from Spain, and those who wanted a heavier Bulldog began to breed to this dog, producing specimens that could weigh up to 100 pounds.

Bulldog fanciers were dismayed to see the cross-breeding of the Bulldog with these very large Spanish-type dogs, and these individuals banded together to form a club, The Bulldog Club. Although the club lasted only a few years, the group did write up the first standard for the breed. As mentioned, another standard was written in 1875, and there are many similarities between these early standards and the present-day standard.

The first dog show with classes for the Bulldog was held in Birmingham, England in 1860. There was one first prize offered for the breed.

The next year, Birmingham again offered the Bulldog class, but this time there was enough interest, with good entries, to warrant first- and second-place prizes. By 1862, the classes were divided by weight between the small-sized Bulldogs and the large dogs, the dividing point usually being 18 pounds. The big winner of these shows was a dog called King Dick, who is considered by many to be the forerunner of the present-day Bulldog type. He was a larger dog, weighing 48 pounds, and red in color, and he handily won the shows of the day.

In the early 1870s, almost all dog shows held various classes for Bulldogs, usually determined by the weight of the dogs. By 1875, the first Bulldog specialty show was held; this became an annual event that still occurs today. By 1879, the show, which took place over a three-day period, consisted of two classes with 76 entries, most of which were considered to be quality Bulldogs. By 1891, the first year that the prestigious English dog show, Crufts, was held, there were

The Bulldog's expression may look imposing, but this is a friendly, affectionate companion breed.

already 50 Bulldog champions in England.

The Bulldog was probably imported into the United States in the 1870s, with the first Bulldog entry at a show in New York City in 1880. The first Bulldog to gain his

CHAPTER 1

American championship was Robinson Crusoe in 1888. C.G. Hopton was the first to breed an American champion. Breeders on the scene at that time, in addition to Mr. Hopton, were John Barnard, James Mortimer, R. Livingston, E.A. Woodward and H.D. Kendall. Mr. Kendall felt that it was important for the breed to bring these individuals together "for the purpose of encouraging the thoughtful and careful breeding of the English Bulldog in America..." All interested fanciers met in

The Bulldog breed had its ups and downs on the way to being the well-established, popular breed it is today.

Boston in 1890 and formed what is now the Bulldog Club of America (BCA).

In addition to being popular in its homeland, England, the Bulldog was now well on its way to becoming a beloved breed in America. By the early 1900s, several wealthy breeders imported top English champions to their kennels, often placing them at public stud at reasonable fees so that the breeders without great wealth to call upon were able to use these dogs and improve their stock.

Through the decades in America, there have been many instrumental breeders, and many outstanding Bullies have been bred and successfully campaigned at dog shows. Although there are too many great ones to discuss in this book, several dogs and breeders should be mentioned here:

Dr. John Saylor of Fearnought Kennels

imported the great Eng. and Am. Ch. Kippax Fearnought. He quickly finished his championship and went Best in Show at the Los Angeles show just ten days after his

Here's Ch. Hetherbull Bounty's Frigate, the top-winning Bulldog, owner-handled by the author.

arrival in the US. In 1954 he won the Non-Sporting Group at the Westminster Kennel Club show and in 1955 he continued his winning ways, going Best in Show at this prestigious show. He won 17 all-breed Bests in Show and continued on to become a great producer.

Karl Foerster and Ray Knudson, using the Smasher

A quality Bulldog is an impressive sight!

prefix, produced many champions, including Ch. Smasher's Al Capp, a Best-in-Show winner who was inducted into the BCA Hall of Fame in 1990. Ch. Marinebull's All The Way, bred by Frank Cox and owned by Karl and Joyce Dingman, became a great Bulldog, winning numerous all-breed Bests in Show and becoming the all-time top producer in the breed at that time with 83 champion offspring. The Dingmans have continued to breed fine Bulldogs under their prefix.

The author and her husband Robert have bred top-quality Bulldogs, including Ch. Hetherbull's Arrogance, sire of 19 champions, and the top-winning Bulldog of all time, Ch. Hetherbull Bounty's Frigate, winner of 52 all-breed Bests in Show and the 1989 BCA national specialty. He is also in the BCA Hall of Fame as a top producer. The Hetheringtons have shown over 100 Bulldogs to their championships.

Mr. and Mrs. Charles Westfield bred and owned Ch. Westfield's Cunemorous Stone, a bitch who was winner of 38 all-breed Bests in Show and 23 specialty shows.

The Bulldog remains a very popular dog in the United States as well as in

England and elsewhere around the world. Within the AKC, where it is classified in the Non-Sporting Group, the Bulldog ranks among the top 20 breeds in popularity according to registration numbers. It places high in popularity in England as well, where it is a member of The Kennel Club's Utility Group.

Although the Bulldog appears as a stocky, heavy dog, don't underestimate his agility, especially when he's got something to celebrate!

MEET THE BULLDOG

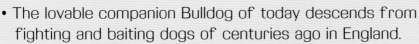

Overview

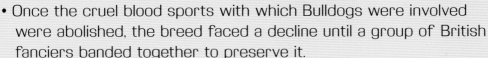

- The lovable companion Bulldog of today descends from fighting and baiting dogs of centuries ago in England.
- Once the cruel blood sports with which Bulldogs were involved were abolished, the breed faced a decline until a group of British fanciers banded together to preserve it.
- Once a breed standard was drawn up and classes at shows were offered for the breed, the Bulldog became a frequent sight in the ring and many earned their championships.
- The Bulldog made its way to the US in the 1870s, where it was welcomed with open arms and developed a dedicated following.
- Thanks to many dedicated breeders, the Bulldog is stabilized and well established as a favorite in many countries around the world.

Description of the Bulldog

E very breed of dog registered with the American Kennel Club has an officially approved breed standard. This is a written account that gives a detailed description of how an ideal representative of the breed should look and act. All breed standards are written up by a committee of national breed club members that is selected by the club. This committee will periodically review the standard to determine if any changes are necessary. Changes are rarely made; when it is determined that there

The head is truly an important feature; in shows, almost 40% of total points awarded are allocated to the head and its features.

should be some changes, it requires considerable discussion and input from club members. The complete Bulldog standard can be found on the American Kennel Club's website (www.akc.org) and on the BCA website (www.thebca.org).

The Bulldog's deep chest makes the legs appear shorter than they really are, although this is by no means a long-legged breed.

The Bulldog is a lively, sturdy, intelligent and confident dog who is very affectionate, devoted, loyal and, of course, very loving. "Kind" and "courageous" are words used to describe him in the standard, which also states that he should not be vicious or aggressive. He has a dignified demeanor and should look very sturdy. This is a medium-sized breed, weighing about 50 pounds for an adult male and 40 pounds for an adult female. The standard notes that, when comparing the two sexes, "due allowance should be made in favor of the bitches, which do not bear the characteristics of the breed to the same degree of perfection and grandeur as do the dogs."

The standard is the "measuring stick" by which dogs are evaluated in the show ring, as well as for breeding potential.

A Bulldog's eyes should be round and of moderate size, neither bulging nor sunken in. The ears are set high on the head. The most desirable ear for the Bulldog is the "rose ear," which is a small drop ear that folds over and back so that the "burr" of the ear (the inside of the ear) is revealed. The Bulldog should have a large black nose; a brown or liver-colored nose is a disqualification from the show ring. Of course, he will have a massive, broad and square jaw with large, strong teeth meeting in an undershot (lower jaw protrudes beyond the upper) bite.

For the show ring, the head of the Bulldog is very important, with 39 points out of 100 allocated to the head and its features. The importance of the head is emphasized when you realize that the same amount of points, 39, is allocated for the entire body, including the neck, legs, feet, tail, etc.

The Bulldog has a short, very thick, deep, strong neck and his body holds a well-rounded rib cage. His topline (line of the back from withers to the rump) differs from that of many breeds, as he has a roach back. This is explained in the standard: "There should be a slight fall in the back, close behind the shoulders, whence the spine

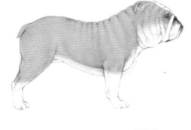

Three of the acceptable colors in the Bulldog, from top to bottom: solid white, red and brindle.

should rise to the loins, thence curving again more suddenly to the tail, forming an arch correctly called the 'wheel back.'" His chest should be broad and deep, which will give the dog a short-legged appearance. The tail may be straight or a screw tail, but it should never be curved or curly. His legs are strong and muscular, with moderately sized feet. He has high knuckles, and his toenails should be kept characteristically short and stubby.

He has a short, flat coat that should be smooth and glossy. The skin is loose all over the body, with heavy wrinkling on the head and face, and a marked dewlap. Bulldogs can be seen in a variety of colors; following is the order of preference: red brindle, all other brindles, solid white, solid red, fawn or fallow, piebald and inferior qualities of the above. Solid black is not desirable.

The Bulldog's gait is all his own: "…a loose-jointed, shuffling, sidewise motion, giving the characteristic 'roll.' The action, must, however, be

John Luke and Daneyko show the true meaning of friendship and the true character of the Bulldog.

unrestrained, free and vigorous."

His ideal temperament is described superbly in the standard: "The disposition should be equable and kind, resolute and courageous (not vicious or aggressive), and demeanor should be pacific and dignified. These attributes should be countenanced by the expression and behavior."

On occasion a breeder will

sell one of his dogs because it does not have acceptable markings or coloration for the show ring or perhaps it has a small fault such as a tail set that is not quite correct.

This does not mean that the dog is not well bred and does not carry the acceptable conformation and temperament of the Bulldog. It simply means that the

Junior Showmanship is sponsored by the AKC and is a wonderful way for aspiring young handlers and their Bulldogs to further their bond.

396 1131

breeder is looking for a dog that more closely meets the ideal for potential showing. A "pet-quality" Bulldog from a good breeder should make a wonderful pet.

Will Judy wrote in the *Dog Encyclopedia* in 1936 about the Bulldog: "The Bulldog makes a most delightful companion and house dog. He is the greatest fraud on earth in that behind his most ferocious look is the gentlest and most kindly disposed nature of any dog...His enormous head, his roach or bended back, his curved legs in front at the elbows, his mushy or wrinkled face, his large soulful eyes, his walk which resembles that of a drunken sailor, his usually attractive color which can be most anything except all black—all these unite to make him a distinctive piece of canine architecture and a breed which those who own swear by."

DESCRIPTION OF THE BULLDOG

Overview

- A breed standard is an official written description of the ideal characteristics, in looks and temperament, for that breed.
- The Bulldog's head is the breed's most impressive feature and one that weighs very heavily in judging.
- The Bulldog is a sturdily built strong dog with a wide chest, thick neck and muscular legs.
- The Bulldog's short coat is seen in a variety of colors. He is known for the heavy wrinkling around his head and face.
- The Bulldog is a friendly, kind and confident dog; a Bulldog should never be aggressive.

Are You a Bulldog Person?

The Bulldog, in spite of his rough-and-tumble roots, is now favored as a companion dog, and this is his only job—to keep his family happy! The Bulldog is a very special and unique breed, each dog with a charming personality all his own. If you decide that you are a suitable owner for a Bulldog, you are sure to be won over by your new family member.

As part of the AKC's Non-Sporting Group of dogs, the Bulldog finds himself keeping company with such

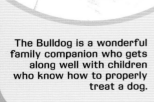

The Bulldog is a wonderful family companion who gets along well with children who know how to properly treat a dog.

breeds as the French Bulldog, Boston Terrier and Miniature and Standard Poodles, other breeds known for their companion-dog qualities. The Bulldog is well known and very recognizable; whenever you are out walking your dog, you will run across someone who will say, with a big smile, "Oh! A Bulldog!"

Follow the leader! Your Bulldog will quickly fall into place as part of the family pack.

Before purchasing your Bulldog, you must think about the personality and characteristics of this breed to determine if this is the dog that you want to join your family. Think about the following questions:

1. Do you have the time to give to a dog? He will need care, companionship, love, training and grooming. This is almost like having a child, except the dog remains childlike in that he will always require your care.

A snuggler beyond compare, your Bulldog is an affectionate companion with whom it is a joy to spend time.

2. Do you have a fenced-in yard for your Bulldog? This is not a breed that you can leave tied out on the porch or to a tree. He must have a

secure area in which to run and exercise.

3. Are you looking for a pet that will be a companion, that will live in the house with you and that will want to spend his waking hours with the family?

4. Have you owned a dog previously and did that dog live a long and happy life with you?

5. Do you have small children and are you willing to train and supervise them so that they will not mistreat their pet?

6. This is a breed that will require little in the way of coat care, but he will need special attention to keeping his skin folds clean. Will you commit yourself to his grooming needs?

7. The Bulldog is a breed that may require extra care because of his "pushed-in" face. Are you willing to take on the special responsibilities of caring for a short-faced dog?

8. Are you looking for a guard dog?

Let's look at the answers to these questions, one at a time:

1. You can work and own a dog, but you will need to plan some time during the day to take care of his needs. Your Bulldog will need quality time spent with you, just like a child. He must be fed on a regular schedule and exercised several times a day. He needs to be hugged and loved, and he will enjoy accompanying you wherever he can. You must work with him to have an obedient dog who has good manners. Your dog should have at least two good outings a day, and that means a walk or a good run in the morning and again in the evening. Walks should be on lead and runs should be in your fenced yard or another securely enclosed area; never let your Bulldog out loose to run the neighborhood.

2. Do you have a fenced-in yard? A yard should give you enough space to play with your dog, to throw a ball and for your dog to run with it. And remember, it is your responsibility to keep the yard clean of

feces. Further, when out walking your dog, it is essential to carry a plastic bag or two to pick up droppings. These can be easily discarded in a handy trash receptacle on your way home.

3. Are you interested in a dog that will be with you, sitting next to you, following you around the house? The Bulldog is not a dog that you can leave alone for hours in the yard and expect him to be content. He is a companion dog, meaning that he expects and needs your companionship and attention.

4. Have you owned a dog previously? This will give you a good idea of what a dog expects from you and what you must do for your dog. All dogs need lessons in manners. The Bulldog is a smart dog, and he likes his owner to be at least as smart as he is!

5. The Bulldog, like many other breeds, is excellent with children, but he needs to be taught how to treat his new young family members, just as the kids must be taught how to treat their dog. They cannot ride on his back, pick him up and drop him, pull his ears or otherwise handle him roughly. When the puppy is brought home, the children must be taught how to pick him up and hold him properly, just as they would be taught with a new baby brother or sister. Interactions between the dog

He may be a little bit bigger than the traditional lap dog, but the Bulldog loves to be near those he loves.

and the kids should always be supervised.

6. Although overall grooming is minimal for this breed, a Bulldog will need to have his coat brushed on a regular basis and have his toenails trimmed, ears and eyes cleaned, wrinkles cleaned and teeth brushed. You will want to make sure that he is kept clean, healthy and smelling good. Are you willing to take the time to do this with your pet?

7. The Bulldog, as well as the Boston Terrier, the French Bulldog, the Boxer and several other breeds, is a brachy-cephalic breed. This means that they have flat faces, wide heads and pushed-in noses. They must have the folds of skin around their eyes and noses cleaned, often on a daily basis. In addition, they are quite susceptible to heat exhaustion and heat stroke and must not be allowed too much time outdoors in heat and humidity. They will require more care, in both the heat and the cold, than will dogs of breeds with regular-length muzzles.

8. The Bulldog is not a guard dog! If this is what you are looking for, you may want to consider another breed, like the Doberman Pinscher or Rottweiler.

The Bulldog is dearly loved for his disposition and his good looks. In addition, he is loved for his intelligence, his devotion to his family and his liveliness. While he does not make a good guard dog, he is watchful, and his looks alone could deter any would-be intruder! Even with all of these positive qualities, you must learn about the breed

Are you ready to do your part in keeping your Bulldog clean and healthy?

before rushing out and buying the first puppy you see.

For more information on the Bulldog, check out other books on the breed and talk to breeders and owners. Bulldog people are happy to give advice about their beloved breed. The Internet can be a wonderful tool as well. Be careful, however, as it's hard to tell what websites contain accurate information. Online sources that you can trust are the Bulldog Club of America, www.thebca.org, and the American Kennel Club, www.akc.org. These sites can also direct you toward Bulldog clubs in your region.

Having done your homework, meaning that you've attended several dog shows, talked to some breeders and done thorough research about Bulldogs, you have now decided that this may be just the right dog for you and your family. Now you are ready to take the next step—finding a reputable and responsible breeder from whom to obtain a puppy.

ARE YOU A BULLDOG PERSON?

Overview

- A Non-Sporting dog by AKC classification, the Bulldog's sole job is to be a family companion.
- Be honest in assessing your lifestyle and your compatibility with the Bulldog breed, as well as your level of commitment to dog ownership as a whole.
- The Bulldog requires special attention to keeping his skin folds clean and to protecting him from weather extremes, as brachycephalic breeds are prone to certain problems.
- Get all the information and advice you can on the Bulldog so you can make a truly educated decision about adding one to your home.

Selecting a Bulldog Breeder

When looking for your new Bulldog puppy, keep in mind that you will be seeking out a healthy puppy from a responsible breeder. A responsible breeder is someone who gives considerable thought before breeding his dogs. He considers health problems in the breed, has room in his home or kennel for a litter of puppies and has the time and dedication to give to a litter. He

Healthy, well-bred puppies come from healthy, well-bred parents who have tested as free of hereditary disorders.

does not breed to the dog down the block because it is easy and he wants to show his children the miracle of birth. The Bulldog is a popular breed and thus attractive to many unethical breeders whose poorly bred pups will likewise be of atypical temperament and poor health. You must be able to recognize a breeder who is profit motivated and not a truly dedicated Bulldog person. Such a person will dismiss your concerns about health problems, sound temperaments, dog shows and up-to-date paperwork.

There's no denying that baby Bulldogs are some of the cutest puppies around!

A responsible breeder, on the other hand, is someone who is dedicated to the breed and to breeding out any faults or hereditary problems, and whose overall interest is in improving the breed. He knows the breed standard well and also knows what to look for in dogs and bitches to be bred. He

Meeting and interacting with the dam and litter is a wonderful education in all of their personalities and a necessary part of the selection process.

will study pedigrees and see what the leading stud dogs are producing. To find the right stud dog for his bitch, he may fly his bitch across the country to breed to a particular stud dog, or may drive the bitch to the dog, who may be located at a considerable distance. However, nowadays breeders can use artificial insemination, so breeders do not always need to send a dog great distances in order to be bred. However, this can be expensive, and the breeder must do thorough research into the breeding pair before attempting artificial insemination.

A good breeder may have only one or two litters a year, which means that there may not be a puppy ready for you when you first call. Whelping a litter is difficult on Bulldog bitches, with the majority undergoing Caesarean sections, so a breeder will not be breeding a particular bitch very often. Be patient, though, and wait for the right puppy from the right breeder.

A breeder/puppy search can be an emotionally trying experience, taxing your patience and your willpower. All Bulldog puppies are adorable, and it's easy to fall in love with the first cute pup you see. But a poor-quality Bulldog will have health and temperament problems that can empty your wallet and break your heart. So do your homework and be prepared before you visit those cute pups! Remember, a reputable breeder is the only source for a Bulldog puppy. Arm yourself with a list of questions for the breeder and be prepared to answer the many questions he will have for you.

To get started on your search, check out the BCA's website to be referred to breeders and affiliated clubs in your region of the country. You will likely be able to find one in your state. The local club should be able to point you toward a responsible breeder or two, as a reputable breeder should belong to the BCA as well as a regional or local club. The clubs are very helpful in that they also will be able to answer any questions that you may have. The responsible Bulldog breeder will probably be someone who has been breeding for some years and someone who is known on the national level.

The responsible breeder will show you his kennel, if he has a kennel, or will invite you into his home to see the puppies. The areas and the puppies will be clean and smell good. The breeder will show you the dam of the litter, and she will be clean and groomed. The sire likely will not be on the premises, but the breeder will show you his photos, pedigree and registration and tell you all about him and why he was chosen to breed with this particular bitch.

The puppies will look healthy and well cared for, with trimmed toenails and clean faces and eyefolds. The breeder may show you only one or two puppies, as he will not show you the puppies that are already sold or that he is going to keep.

A Bulldog puppy should be a solid, sturdy youngster with a clean coat, healthy skin and a friendly, alert temperament.

Ask to see the registration papers and pedigrees of the sire and dam. Although AKC registration is no guarantee of quality, it is one small step in the right direction. If you hope to show your pup or enter licensed competitions, registration with the AKC is necessary. The pedigree should include three to five generations of ancestry. Inquire about any titles in the pedigree. Titles indicate a dog's accomplishments in some area of canine competition, which proves the merits of the ancestors and adds to the breeder's credibility. You should see "Ch." in a show puppy's pedigree, indicating that a relative was a champion. While it is true that, like the registration, a pedigree cannot guarantee health or good temperament, a well-constructed pedigree is still a good starting point. There should be no extra fee, by the way, for either the pedigree or registration papers. The AKC states that papers do not cost extra, and any breeder who charges for those documents is unscrupulous.

Ask about health issues and clearances. Bulldogs are prone to hip dysplasia, a potentially crippling joint disease. Do the

sire and dam have hip clearances from the OFA (Orthopedic Foundation for Animals, a national canine genetic-disease registry)? The Bulldog can also suffer from health problems common to short-faced breeds, including elongated soft palate, entropion and ectropion (eyelid abnormalities), muzzle pyoderma and wrinkle dermatitis. Ask the breeder about these problems and their frequency of occurrence in his line and the breed in general.

Most reputable breeders have a puppy sales contract that includes specific health guarantees and reasonable health-related return policies. Your breeder should also agree to accept a puppy back if things do not work out. He should be willing, indeed anxious, to check up on the puppy's progress after the pup goes home with you and should be available if you have questions or problems with the pup.

Puppies are protected from common canine diseases for their first weeks of life due to the protective colostrum found in their mother's milk.

The breeder will have an adoption application and many questions for you. Have you had a dog before? How many have you had and have you ever owned a Bulldog? Did your dogs live long lives and do you have a fenced yard? How many children do you have and what are their ages? Are you willing to spend the time to teach your children in how to treat the new family member? Have you ever done any dog training and are you willing to go to obedience classes with your dog? Are there any other pets in your household? You should not be offended by the breeder's questions, as he has the breed's best interests in mind. Plus, he has put a lot of time, effort and money into this litter, and his first priority is to place each pup in a caring and appropriate household where the pup will be wanted, loved and cared for.

SELECTING A BULLDOG BREEDER

Overview

- Know what to look for in a reputable breeder and how to recognize warning signs that a person is less than ethical in his breeding practices.
- Consult reliable sources like the Bulldog Club of America and AKC in your breeder search and be sure that the breeder's standards are what you would expect.
- The breeder will likewise have many questions for you and only agree to sell you a pup if he trusts that you will make a worthy owner.
- When visiting the litter, you should see where the dogs are kept, meet the dam and other dogs on the premises, see the litter's and parents' health certifications and discuss terms of the sale.
- A good breeder will be a source of support throughout your Bulldog's lifetime with you.

Finding the Right Puppy

If you are ready to commit to owning a puppy, you are now ready to make your pick. You have decided that the Bulldog is the dog that you want to and can live with and enjoy. Your entire family is ready for bringing this new arrival into your home and lives. You have done your homework and have located a responsible breeder who has a litter available.

Before seeing the breeder and his pups, you should give some consideration to the type of puppy that you

Although this Bulldog puppy has a lot of growing to do, his build and features resemble those of an adult Bulldog in miniature.

want. For example, are you looking for a male or for a female puppy? Some individuals consider males easier to train but the more dominant of the two sexes; others prefer the softer disposition of a female. In some breeds, females become adults as soon as they have their first heat cycles, and males remain puppy-like for their first several years. There are a few points that should be considered in making your decision. In the Bulldog, size will make a difference as, in general, females are about ten pounds lighter than males. Females should also look more feminine than males.

These puppies are much too young for visitors. They will receive all of the care and early socialization that they need from their attentive breeder.

If you do not plan to neuter/spay your pet (and some breeders will require you to neuter your dog or spay your bitch if the dog is not to be shown or bred), a female will come into season (heat) approximately every six months. This can be a difficult time that lasts for up to three

One thing's for sure about all Bulldog puppies—they are irresistible!

CHAPTER 5

weeks. It is fairly messy and hard on the house, and it will attract any wandering males in the neighborhood, who will sit on your doorstep like lovelorn swains. Males who are not neutered can be more headstrong and will have more of a tendency to lift their legs and to mount yours. Discuss this with the breeder

Meeting the litter is the fun part! Get right in the middle of the puppy pack as you get to know each pup's personality and see to which one you feel most attracted.

if you are not sure which sex you want; he can give you some advice.

As soon as you look at your first litter of Bulldog puppies you will realize that Bulldog puppies are as cute as they come! When you arrive at the breeder's home, you

should see a happy bunch of clean and healthy puppies. Their noses will be wet, their coats will have a glow and they will have a nice covering of flesh over their ribs. They should be bouncing around, happy to see you, and you will be ready to pick up one of these rascals and cuddle him in your arms.

When looking over the pups, you will likely find the puppy that hangs back as well as the extra-active, most outgoing of the litter. In general, though, Bulldog puppies may not be as hyper as puppies of other breeds. If you do meet a hyper puppy, remember that hyper puppies can turn into hyper adults and will require more patience and time in training. The most shy pup in the litter and the most outgoing will likely present challenges, so you should look for the middle-of-the-road puppy, the one that is interested, comes up to you, listens when you speak and looks very alert.

Never, but never, pick the pup that hangs back and will not come up to you. Never pick a puppy because you "feel sorry" for him. Don't forget—you are adding a new member to your family and you want one that is bright, healthy and sound. Find the bright-eyed, alert puppy with the sparkling eyes and extroverted disposition.

If this is your first experience with puppy ownership, do know that there will be expenses in addition to the price of the puppy. You will need leashes, dog dishes and grooming utensils. You will need safe chew toys and clean-up supplies for the inevitable potty accidents. A wire dog crate is essential as well as a fenced-in yard. There will be

food to buy and veterinary expenses. The breeder will give you documentation to take home with the pup, including his registration papers, pedigree, health records and copy of his sales

When you find the perfect pup for you, you will know it!

contract. He will probably also give you some care instructions, a diet sheet and perhaps some of the food that puppy has been eating. Before purchasing the pup, you must be confident that you are bringing home a sound companion and that you can rely on your breeder for support.

ADOPTING AN ADULT

Aside from buying a puppy, there is another way to add a Bulldog to your life and that is to adopt a "rescue" Bulldog. This will be a dog who, for a wide variety of reasons, is in need of a new home. Often the dog will be over one year of age and very often he is trained and housebroken to some extent. The breed rescue organization, which is usually affiliated with the national or another Bulldog club, will have a network of foster homes where the dogs live with families, awaiting adoptions into new permanent homes. The rescue organization will have the dogs checked by the vet, providing veterinarians' health certificates attesting to the health of the dogs. The foster families give the dogs love, attention and social-ization while awaiting adoption. Often these dogs make marvelous pets, as they are grateful for a second chance at a loving home.

Not only does the national club have an active rescue organization, but local clubs will also have groups of individuals working in this area. Rescue committees consist of very dedicated individuals who care deeply about the breed and give countless hours of their time and money to assure that each dog will have an equal chance in life. The BCA's rescue network has rescuers and coordinators across the US and in Canada as well. While you will want to inves-tigate the background of a rescue dog as much as possible by going through the Bulldog Club of America's rescue organization, you should be assured of getting a dog that you will be able to live with. A link to the BCA's rescue organization and a state-by-state list of contacts can be found at www.thebca.org.

Another adoption option

is that the breeder may have an older dog that he wants to place in a good pet home. For some breeders, once they have put a championship on a dog, they would like to move this animal into a home where he will receive the optimum of attention as a companion dog. Do give this some thought, as often an older dog will be trained and easy to live with.

TEMPERAMENT TESTING

You should ask the breeder if the sire and dam of the litter have had their temperaments tested. These are tests that are offered by the American Temperament Test Society (ATTS); responsible breeders will be familiar with this organization. The breeder will show you the score sheet and you can easily determine if the parents of the litter have the types of personalities that you are looking for. In addition, this is an excellent indication that this is a

responsible breeder.

Temperament testing by the ATTS is done on dogs that are at least 18 months of age; therefore puppies are not tested, but the sire and dam of a litter can be tested. The test is like a simulated walk

If you are sure that you want a Bulldog, but wary of raising a puppy, consider adding an adolescent or adult to your family. There are many deserving dogs out there in need of loving homes.

through a neighborhood where everyday situations are encountered. Neutral, friendly and threatening situations are encountered to observe the dog's reactions to the various stimuli. Problems that are looked for are unprovoked

CHAPTER 5

aggression, panic without recovery and strong avoidance. The testers watch the dog's behavior toward strangers, reactions to auditory, visual and tactile stimuli and self-protective and aggressive behavior. The dog is on a loose lead for the test, which takes about ten minutes to complete. Recent ATTS statistics show 119 Bulldogs having been tested

Leaving mom's side to become part of a human pack is a big step for a small pup, but all he needs to make the transition is lots of love.

in one year, with only 68.1% having a passing rate. This is a fairly low rate when compared to most breeds, which serves to further stress the importance of purchasing a Bulldog puppy with a good, steady temperament from a reputable breeder.

Some breeders will have the temperaments of their puppies tested by either a professional behaviorist, a veterinarian or another dog breeder. These tests will find the high-energy pup and the pup that will be slower in responding, as well as the pup with the independent spirit and the one that will want to follow the pack. Whether or not the litter has been tested, the breeder will still know the pups well and be able to suggest which pup he thinks will be best for your family.

If the litter has not been tested, you can do a few simple tests while you are sitting on the floor, playing with the pups. Pat your leg or snap your finger and see which pup comes up to you first. Clap your hands and see if one of the pups shies away from you. Watch how they play with one another. The puppy whose personality appeals to you most is probably the puppy that you will take home. Remember, you are looking for the puppy that appears to be "in the middle," not overly rambunctious, aggressive or submissive. You want a joyful pup, not a wild one.

Spend some time observing the pups and consider your decision carefully. If you are hesitant, tell the breeder that you would like to go home and think over your choice. A good breeder will not pressure you into buying a puppy immediately. This is a major decision, as you are adding a family member who should be with for the next decade, hopefully longer, so you want to be sure to get a puppy that you will all be happy with.

FINDING THE RIGHT PUPPY

Overview

- What are you looking for in a Bulldog puppy? Be sure to communicate this clearly to the breeder to aid him in guiding you to the perfect match.
- When you visit the litter, look for health, soundness and temperament in the whole litter, not just the pup you are considering.
- Don't be overwhelmed by puppy cuteness. Carefully consider your choice as well as whether you are ready for everything that goes along with puppy ownership.
- If you want a Bulldog but not sure about raising a puppy, think about adopting a rescued adult Bulldog or one who's retired from the show ring.
- Learn as much as you can about your prospect's temperament, whether through formal testing, observations, the breeder's advice or a combination of these.

Welcoming the Bulldog Puppy

You have selected your puppy and are ready to bring your new family member home. Before your pup's arrival, you must have the necessities in place; this includes puppy food, food and water bowls, a crate, a leash, a collar and an ID tag with your contact information on it. Your puppy will not only sleep in the crate but also will spend time in the crate when you are at work or out on errands, or when you otherwise cannot supervise him. In very short order your puppy will learn that the crate is his second

Have some sturdy puppy toys on hand to keep those teeth busy and out of trouble!

"home," and he will feel safe and secure when he is in his crate. A pup who is left out loose in the house by himself can quickly find all kinds of things to keep him "busy," such as chewing on the furniture as well as the corners of woodwork. As well as being destructive, puppy's ways of occupying himself are certain to be dangerous to him as well. Keep him in a confined area when you cannot watch him and you can eliminate these problems. Be sure to put several towels or a washable blanket in the crate so that he will be cozy and comfortable. Here is a short rundown of the puppy necessities that you should have on hand for your Bulldog pup:

Remember that your new pup is making a big transition away from his familiar breeder, mother and littermates, so he will need some time to adjust.

Food and water bowls: Breeders recommend stainless steel bowls, as plastic bowls will be chewed up in short order. Further, Bulldogs do best with bowls or pans that have straight sides and flat bottoms.

Your attention and gentle handling will help puppy acclimate and bond with you. In no time, he will be feeling right at home!

Collar: A buckle collar is good for everyday use; this should have puppy's ID tags, dog licenses, etc., attached to it with a secure "O" ring. For walks, a chain choke collar with small links is suggested.

Leash: A lightweight lead is all that the Bulldog puppy will need. As he grows larger and stronger, he will need a thicker, stronger leash as well.

Crate: A wire crate is a must for the Bulldog, as wire crates offer good ventilation. The short-faced Bulldog will not do well in a fiberglass crate with limited ventilation. Also have some padding for the crate. Initially the crate can be lined with towels, as they are easily washable in case potty accidents occur.

Toys: Bulldogs need strong toys as both puppies and adults. You will increase the size of the toys as the dog grows, making sure that they do not have pieces that can be chewed off and that they are too large to be swallowed.

Strong nylon and hard rubber bones are good for Bulldogs; rawhide chews are not, so avoid them altogether.

Grooming equipment: A soft-bristle brush and nail clippers are essential for the pup, as well as washcloths and cotton wipes for cleaning the ears, eyes and wrinkles. A grooming table is optional but can be a helpful piece of equipment.

Wire pen and/or baby gates: Called an "ex-pen," a wire pen is helpful for confining your pup in a larger area than his crate. Likewise, baby gates can block a doorway to keep puppy in a designated puppy-proofed room or area.

If you are driving some distance to pick up your Bulldog puppy, take along a towel or two, a water bowl and your pup's leash and collar. Also take along some plastic baggies and a roll of paper towels in case there are any potty accidents or motion sickness along the way.

Before bringing your puppy into the house, you should be aware that there are dangers in the household that must be eliminated. Electrical wires should be raised off the floor and hidden from view, as they are very tempting as chewable objects. Swimming pools can be very dangerous, particularly for Bulldogs with their short legs and heavy bodies, as it will be difficult if not impossible for them to climb out of a pool. Make certain that your puppy can't get into, or fall into, the pool. Sturdy barricades will be necessary to prevent an accident. Likewise, watch your deck railings and make sure that your puppy cannot slip through the openings and fall.

As we've discussed, any children in the family must understand that the small puppy is a living being that must be treated gently. This is your responsibility! A child taught about animals at an

Confinement for your puppy is necessary for his safety and to keep him from too much puppy mischief as he's learning the rules of the roost.

early age can become a compassionate animal lover and owner.

Use your common sense in all of the aforementioned safety situations. Consider where a young child can get into trouble, and your puppy will be right behind him!

After puppy has relieved himself and when he comes into the house for the first time, let your pup look at his new home and surroundings, and give him a light meal and a pan of water. When he is tired, take him outside again and then tuck him into his

CHAPTER 6

crate, either to take a nap or, hopefully, to sleep through the night.

The first day or two for your puppy should be fairly quiet. He will then have time to get used to his new home, surroundings and family members. The first night, he may cry a bit, but if you put a teddy bear or a soft, woolly sweater in his crate, this will

You control what your puppy puts in his mouth. Supervise him and be ready with a safe chew toy lest he turn his attention to your belongings or something that could do him harm.

give him some warmth and security. A nearby ticking clock or a radio playing soft music can also be helpful. Remember, he has been uprooted from a sibling or two, his mother and his familiar breeder, and he will

need a day or two to get used to his new family. If he should cry during this first night, let him be. He will eventually quiet down and sleep. By the third night, he should be well settled in. Have patience and, within a week or less, it will seem to you, your family and your puppy that you have all been together for years.

Routine is very important for a puppy, so you should start him on a feeding schedule from day one. This will help in the house-training routine as well. Your young puppy will probably be fed three times a day, perhaps as many as four times a day, to start. As he grows, you will eventually cut his meals to two times a day, in the morning and in the evening. Avoid feeding table scraps and keep in mind that certain "people foods," like chocolate, nuts, raisins, grapes and onions, are toxic to dogs. Use dog treats wisely in training and give him a treat at bedtime. Keep a good covering of flesh over his ribs, but do not let your young Bulldog become a fat puppy! However, the more active the dog, the more calories he will need. Always have fresh drinking water available. This should include a bowl of water in the kitchen and another outside in the yard, remembering to change the water often.

You are now off to an excellent start with your puppy. He will be settling in nicely and, as the days go by, you will figure out which additional items that you need. For example, as your puppy learns how to walk on a leash politely, you will likely want a longer, possibly a retractable, leash for walks in the park. Your pup will appreciate having a larger area to sniff and explore. You may want to invest in a dog bed once you think your pup won't chew it up or make a puddle on it. These items can be acquired as needed from your local pet shop.

WELCOMING THE BULLDOG PUPPY

Overview

- Before your pup comes home, you must prepare your house with the necessary puppy accessories and by making it safe and puppy-proof.
- Puppy food, food and water bowls, a leash, a collar, ID tags, grooming supplies and a crate are among the items you will need for your Bulldog pup.
- All family members should be prepared for the new arrival, making his arrival low-key and being sure to handle him gently.
- Start your pup on a routine as soon as he comes home. The sooner you begin, the sooner he will learn.

CHAPTER 7

House-training and Other Basics

You choose your puppy's relief site. If you have a fenced yard, he will learn to locate it on his own after a few times of your leading him there.

Habits, and that includes good and bad habits, that are learned at an early age become lifelong habits, so it is best to start out on the right foot. For example, don't let your puppy chew on the leg of the old kitchen chair and think that it's cute, because before long he will have chewed up the leg of your expensive dining-room table. Set limits, be consistent in enforcing them and make sure that puppy sticks to them.

Keep your pup to a schedule as much as you can and he will become schedule-oriented very quickly, which is helpful for you, too. If puppy gets used to the routine of hearing you get up at 7:00 every morning and then going outside with you a few minutes later, he will learn to wait for you to let him out rather than relieving himself in his crate.

Keep your puppy confined to a specific area, such as the kitchen or den, until he is trained and fairly mature. Use baby gates and he will quickly learn that he is welcomed in certain areas of the house and not in other areas. Of course, put him in his crate when you leave him home alone, as he will be comfortable and safe in his own personal "house." It will take the pup a little time to get used to his crate, but in no time he will learn to settle down and rest until you return.

A very important factor in training a young pup is to give him a name. Sometimes it may take a week or so before you find a name that fits the

Once your dog is reliably house-trained, his potty routine will be just another part of your day.

Newspapers can be useful in the initial stages of house-training, progressing to your ultimate goal of training him to relieve himself outdoors.

dog; other times, you will have him named before you even bring him home. We have had several pets who've had their names changed a week or two after coming home, as the original names did not quite "fit" their personalities. In general, short one- or two-syllable names are the easiest for training, such as "No, Sam." It becomes more difficult when you have to say, "No, Russell John" or "Sit, Mary Beth Rose." You want a name that not only fits the personality of the dog but one that fits the breed itself. For example, a German-sounding name like Bruno or Klaus is not as fitting for a Bulldog as something more British, like Humphrey or Churchill. Use his name often, popping him a treat when he looks at you, and your dog will quickly know that you are talking about him.

Your dog must be house-trained. This job should begin as soon as you bring your pup home—do not think that you can delay! Diligence during the first two or three weeks will surely pay off. House-training a Bulldog should be a relatively easy task, since the breed is quick to learn, but much of your puppy's success depends on you!

Every time your puppy wakes up from a nap, he should be quickly taken outside. Watch him and praise him with "Good boy!" when he urinates or defecates. Give him a pat on the head and take him back inside after he's relieved himself. All puppies have a few accidents, but with a firm "No" from you at the appropriate time (catch him in the act!) he will quickly learn that it is better to go outside to do his "job" than to do it on the kitchen floor and be scolded. If you do catch him relieving himself indoors, give a firm "No" right away, then pick him up and bring him outdoors to the chosen relief spot to finish his business.

You will soon learn the habits of your dog. However, at the following times it is essential to take your puppy out: when he gets up in the morning, after he eats, before he goes to bed, after long naps and any time he looks like he's sniffing out a place to "go." A young puppy may need more than ten potty trips a day, but most adult dogs will only have to go out three or four times a day. Some dogs will go to the door and bark when they want to be let out, and others will nervously circle around. Watch and learn from his signs, and don't ignore the signals he gives you.

Crates are a major help in house-training, as most dogs will not want to dirty their living quarters. The crate is actually a multi-purpose dog accessory: your Bulldog's personal dog house within your house, a humane house-training tool, a security measure that will protect your household and belongings when you're not home, a travel aid to house and protect your dog when you are traveling (most motels will accept a crated dog) and,

Crate-training when your Bulldog is a puppy results in an adult who's happy to have a private den of his own.

finally, a comfy dog space for your puppy when your anti-dog relatives come to visit. Some experienced breeders insist on crate use after their puppies leave, and a few even begin to crate-train their pups before they send them home. But it's more likely that your pup has never seen a crate, so it's up to you to make sure his

CHAPTER 7

introduction to the crate is a pleasant one.

Introduce the crate as soon as he comes home so he learns that this is his new "house." This is best accomplished with dog treats. For the first day or two, toss a tiny treat into the crate to entice him to go in. Pick a crate command, such as "Kennel," "Inside" or "Crate," and use it every time he enters. You also can feed his first few meals inside the crate with the door still open, so the crate association will be a happy one.

Your puppy should sleep in his crate from his very first night. He may whine at first and object to the confinement, but be strong! If you release him when he cries, you provide his first life lesson…if I cry, I get out and maybe hugged. A better scheme is to place the crate next to your bed at night for the first few weeks. Your presence will comfort him, and you'll also know if he needs a midnight potty trip.

A house-trained dog is a dog that can have more freedom in the home with no worries of accidents.

Whatever you do, do not lend comfort by taking the puppy into bed with you. To a dog, on the bed means equal, which is not a good idea this early on, as you're trying to establish your leadership.

Make a practice of placing your puppy in his crate for naps, at nighttime and whenever you are unable to watch him closely. Not to worry…he will let you know when he wakes up and needs a potty trip. Think of what would happen if he were uncrated. He would wake up, make a puddle and then toddle over to say "Hi!"

Routines, consistency and an eagle eye are your keys to house-training success. Remember that puppies always "go" when they wake up, within a few minutes after eating, after play periods and after brief periods of confinement. Always lead the puppy on his leash outside to the same area, telling him "Outside" as you go out. If you have a fenced yard,

Follow your nose! A dog's sense of smell is what leads him to find a suitable place to relieve himself.

eventually you will be able to let pup out on his own and he will find his spot.

Pick a "potty" word, (like "Hurry up," "Go potty" and "Get busy") and use it when he does his business, lavishing "Good puppy!" praise on him, repeating your potty word. Use the same exit door for these potty trips, and confine puppy to the exit area so he can find it when he needs it. Again, don't ignore his signs! Don't allow him to roam the house until he's house-trained; how will he find that outside door if he's three or four rooms away?

If puppy has an accident, never rub your puppy's nose in his mistake or strike your puppy or adult dog with your hand, a newspaper or other object to correct him. He will not understand and will only become fearful of the person who is hitting him.

House-training hint: remove the puppy's water after 7:00 at night to aid in nighttime bladder control. If he gets thirsty, offer him an ice cube. Then just watch him race for the refrigerator when he hears the rattle of the ice cube tray.

Despite its many benefits, crate use can be abused. Puppies under 12 weeks of age should never be confined for more than two hours at a time, unless, of course, they are sleeping. A general rule of thumb is three hours

Taking your pup outside on his leash for potty trips means that you will be one step ahead when it comes to teaching the basic commands.

maximum for a three-month-old pup, four to five hours for the four- to five-month-old and no more than six hours for dogs over six months of age. If you're unable to be home to release the dog, arrange for a relative, neighbor or dogsitter to let him out to exercise and potty.

One final, but most important, rule of crate use: never, ever, use the crate for punishment. Successful crate use depends on your puppy's positive association with his "house." If the crate repre-sents punishment or "bad dog stuff," he will resist using it as his safe place. Sure, you can crate your pup after he has sorted through the trash. Just don't do it in an angry fashion or tell him "Bad dog, crate!"

Be patient with the house-training, as this can sometimes be a trying time. It is simply essential to have a clean house dog, and life will be much easier for all of you—not to mention for the carpeting, too!

HOUSE-TRAINING AND OTHER BASICS

Overview

- All family members must agree upon the rules for the pup and be consistent in enforcing them.
- Along with pup's crate, baby gates are effective in creating a safe area for puppy confinement to aid in house-training and safety.
- Pick an appropriate, easy-to-say name that fits your pup's personality.
- House-training is based on diligence and consistency. Take your pup out often, to the same area, and get to know the signals he gives when he needs to go out.
- The crate, when used properly, is an effective tool in the house-training process.

Puppy Lessons and Commands

Dogs are pack animals; as such, they need a leader. Your Bulldog's first boss was his mother, and all of his life lessons came from his mom and littermates. Now you have to assume the role of leader and communicate appropriate behavior in terms his little canine mind will understand. Remember, too, that from a canine perspective, human rules make no sense at all.

When you start the teaching process, remember that the first 20 weeks of any canine's life are his most valuable learning time, a period

Anything tastes good to a teething pup, but nipping is unacceptable behavior that must be "nipped" in the bud.

when his mind is best able to soak up every lesson, both positive and negative. Positive experiences and proper socialization during this period are critical to his future development and stability. Do you want a well-behaved dog or a naughty dog? It's up to you.

Canine behavioral science tells us that any behavior that is rewarded will be repeated. That's called positive reinforcement. If something good happens, like a tasty treat or hugs and kisses, a puppy will naturally want to repeat the behavior. That same research also has proven that one of the best ways to a puppy's mind is through his stomach. Never underestimate the power of a treat!

Have treats on hand and be prepared to reinforce good behavior whenever it occurs. That same reinforcement principle also applies to undesirable behavior, like digging in the trash can, which the dog or

Your puppy's optimal age for learning is when you first bring him home. You can begin teaching him simple basic commands like "Sit."

Puppy must learn what he can and cannot chew on for his own safety. Many an injury has occurred due to puppy-chewed electrical cords, so be preventive and fasten them against the wall or floor where pup cannot get to them.

puppy does not know is "wrong." It's fun for the pup, so why not? What better reason to keep a sharp eye on your puppy so you can catch him in the act and tell him "No" to prevent those normal canine behaviors? By showing him what behaviors are wrong, and popping him a treat when he stops the undesirable behavior, he learns what is considered "bad" and learns that being good has its rewards.

Gentle guidance will show your puppy what you expect of him when you issue the sit command.

BASIC COMMANDS

You must have a mannerly dog; therefore, your Bulldog's knowledge of some basic commands will make him a better canine citizen. If you and puppy attend a puppy class, you will probably cover some introductory lessons and then move on to the important basics: sit, heel, down, come (recall) and stay. If you attend training classes, you will have professional help in learning these commands, but you and your pup can learn and practice these basic exercises on your own at home. Teach all commands initially with your Bulldog on leash; attempt off-leash exercises only in a safely enclosed area.

Sit

This is the first and simplest exercise to teach. Place your dog on your left side as you are standing and say "Sit" firmly. As you say this, run your hand down your dog's back and gently guide him into a sitting position. Praise him, hold him in this position for a few moments, release your hand, praise him again and give him a treat. Repeat this several times a day, perhaps as many as ten times. It also helps to raise the treat

him. Have your dog sit on your left side and, as you say "Stay," place your hand in front of his nose and walk around from his side to stand in front of him, facing him. Take a step or two away, no more at the beginning, using your hand

No matter how near to or how far away from the dog you are when practicing the stay command, always use the hand signal along with the word "Stay."

above the dog's head; as he looks up at the treat, his backside will naturally go to the floor. Before long, your pup will understand what you want; pups learn the sit command quickly.

Stay

Teach your dog to stay in a seated position until you call

signal and repeating the verbal command "Stay." After ten seconds or so, call your dog to you. If he gets up before the end of the command, have him sit again and repeat the stay command. When he stays until called, (remembering to start with a very short period of time), praise him and give him a treat. As he learns this command, increase the space that you move away from the dog as well as the length of time that he stays.

Heel

The formal heel command comes a bit later in the learning curve. A young Bulldog should be taught simply to walk politely on a leash, at or near your side. That is best accomplished when your pup is very young and small, instead of a

Teaching polite manners to your Bulldog pup will pay off when you have an adult who walks nicely by your side, not pulling in all directions.

strong adult pulling you down the street.

Start leash training soon after your pup comes home. Simply attach his leash to his buckle collar and let him drag it around for a little while every day. Play a puppy game with the leash on. Make wearing his leash a happy moment in his day. If he chews the leash, distract him with a play activity.

After a few days, you will be ready to try walking together. For this you will want to put the small choke collar on the pup. Be sure that you have been shown how to put it on and use it properly. Hold a treat lure at his eye level to encourage him to walk next to you. Pat your knee and use a happy voice. Use the phrase "Let's go!" as you move forward, holding the treat low to keep him near. Take a few steps, give the treat and praise. Move forward just a few steps each time.

Keep these sessions short

and happy, a mere 30 seconds at a time (that's long in puppy time). Never pull on the lead, thus dragging him around with the choke collar; rather, just encourage him with happy talk. Walk straight ahead at first, adding wide turns once he gets the hang of it. Progress to 90° turns, a happy verbal "Let's go!" and, of course, a treat. You will always use only gentle leash tugs so that the choke collar quickly releases after tightening. Walk in short 10- to 20-second bursts with a happy break (use a release word like "Okay") and brief play (hugs will do nicely) in between. Always quit with success, even if just a few short steps.

Down

This will probably be the most complicated of the five basic commands to teach, as dogs view the down position as a submissive one. Place your dog in the sit position, kneel down next to him and place your right hand under his front legs and your left hand on his shoulders. As you say "Down," gently push his front legs out into the down position. As soon as his elbows reach the floor, give him a treat, talk gently to him, stroke

his back so that he will be comfortable and then praise him. Once he knows the down well, you can teach him to stay in the down position using the same method as with the sit/stay.

A little hand pressure will help your Bulldog assume the down position, but never be forceful.

Come

The recall, or come command, is probably the most important for your dog's safety. If your dog escapes

CHAPTER 8

from the yard, breaks his leash or otherwise gets away from you or is nosing around in something harmful, his reliable response to your call could save his life. Always practice the come command on leash and in a safely confined area. You can't afford to risk failure or the pup will learn he does not have to come when called, and you want his response to be reliable.

Once you have the pup's attention, call him from a short distance: "Puppy, come!" Use your happy voice and give a treat when he comes to you. If he hesitates, tug him to you gently with his leash. Grasp and hold his collar with one hand as you dispense the treat. The collar grasp is important. You will eventually phase out the treat and switch to hands-on praise only. This maneuver also connects holding his collar with coming and treating, which will assist you in countless future behaviors.

Do 10 or 12 repetitions 2 or 3 times a day. Once your pup has mastered "Come," continue to practice daily to imprint this most important behavior into his puppy brain. Experienced dog owners know, however, that one can never completely trust a dog to come when called if he is bent on a self-appointed mission. Off leash is often synonymous with out of control. For his safety, always keep your Bulldog on leash when not in a fenced or confined area.

When training outdoors, be prepared to deal with puppy distractions! A stick, an insect, a leaf blowing by—most anything can take his mind off the lesson.

A very important note: never tell your dog to come to you and then correct him for something he did wrong. He will think the correction is for coming to you (think like a dog, remember?) and will hesitate to come to you in the future if he thinks he's going to be scolded. Always greet his coming to you with happy praise and petting. Always go to the dog to stop unwanted behavior, but be sure you catch him in the act or your correction will not be understood correctly.

KEEP PRACTICING

An important part of training is patience, persistence and routine. Remember to teach each command the same way every time and reward him for performing commands correctly. Continue with short practice sessions throughout the dog's lifetime and integrate his commands into your daily routine. You will certainly appreciate your dog's good manners, and so will visitors to your home and everyone you meet.

PUPPY LESSONS AND COMMANDS

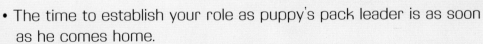

Overview

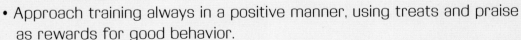

- The time to establish your role as puppy's pack leader is as soon as he comes home.
- Approach training always in a positive manner, using treats and praise as rewards for good behavior.
- Among the basic commands for your Bulldog's training and safety are sit, stay, heel, down and come.
- Practice makes perfect! Reinforce your Bulldog's basic training with daily practice and incorporating the exercises into the daily routine.

Home Care of Your Bulldog

The Bulldog's average lifespan is about ten years, hopefully longer. The quality of those years depends on a conscientious home healthcare program. Although genetics and the environment certainly can influence a dog's longevity, the fact remains that you are the backbone of your Bulldog's health-maintenance program. Like the proverbial apple a day, your daily focus on canine wellness will help "keep the veterinarian away."

The two most important health regimens are, without a moment's doubt, weight control and dental

To keep your Bulldog a happy, healthy member of the family, you must be his "home healthcare provider" in between veterinary visits.

hygiene. Veterinarians tell us that over 50% of the dogs they see are grossly overweight and that such obesity will take two to three years off a dog's life, given the strain it puts on the animal's heart, lungs and joints. The obvious message here: lean is healthier!

If left to his own devices, the treat jar would be empty! Use your Bulldog's love of food to your advantage in training, but do it prudently!

WEIGHT CONTROL

If your Bulldog could suddenly speak, the first thing that he would say is "Who are you calling a chow-hound?" No Bulldog has ever been accused of having a poor appetite! To determine if your Bulldog is overweight, you should be able to feel your dog's ribs beneath a thin layer of muscle with very gentle pressure on his rib cage. When viewing your dog from above, you should be able to see a definite waistline, and from the side he should have an obvious tuck-up in his abdomen. True, the Bulldog is a solid, stocky dog, but there is a

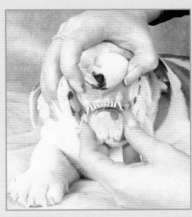

Your dog's teeth need to be brushed just as yours do. An often-overlooked but extremely essential component of a dog's care is regular attention to his dental hygiene at home.

definite difference between a Bulldog in muscular condition and one that is overweight. Keep a record of your dog's weight from each annual vet visit. A few extra pounds? Adjust his food portions, decrease the amount of treats, perhaps switch to a "light," "senior" or lower calorie dog-food formula and increase his exercise. A weight-loss program should be discussed with your vet.

Excessive weight is especially hard on older dogs with creaky joints. A senior Bulldog who is sedentary will grow out of shape more quickly. Walking (slower for old guys) is still the best workout for health maintenance. Tailor your dog's exercise to fit his age and physical condition.

ORAL HYGIENE

Now let's examine your dog's teeth. The American Veterinary Dental Society states that 80% of dogs show signs of oral disease as early as age three.

Further studies prove that good oral hygiene can add three to five years to a dog's life, so look at your dog's teeth right away. Danger signs include yellow and brown build-up of tartar along the gumline, inflamed red gums and persistent bad breath. If neglected, these conditions will allow bacteria to accumulate in your dog's mouth and enter his blood-stream through those damaged gums, increasing the risk for disease in vital organs such as the heart and liver. It's also known that periodontal disease is a major contributor to kidney disease, which is a common cause of death in older dogs...and preventable.

Your vet should examine your Bulldog's teeth and gums during his annual checkup to make sure they are clean and healthy. He may recommend a professional cleaning if there is excessive plaque build-up. During the other 364 days of the year, you are your dog's dentist. Brush his teeth daily, or at least twice a week. Use a doggie toothbrush (designed for the contour of a canine's mouth) and use dog toothpaste flavored with chicken, beef or liver. (Minty people paste is harmful to dogs.) If your dog resists a toothbrush, try a nappy washcloth or gauze pad wrapped around your finger. Start the brushing process with gentle gum massages when your Bulldog is very young so he will learn to tolerate and even enjoy the process.

Feeding dry dog food is an excellent way to help minimize plaque accumulation. You can also treat your dog to a raw carrot every day. Carrots help scrub away plaque while providing extra vitamins A and C. Invest in healthy chew objects, such as nylon or hard rubber bones and toys with ridges that act as tartar scrapers. Specially designed dental bones will help to remove and prevent plaque. Raw beef knuckle bones (cooked bones will splinter) also work, but watch for sharp edges and splintering on these or any other chew object, which can cut the dog's mouth and intestinal lining. Rawhides are not recommended for Bulldogs.

CHECKING OVER THE COAT

Your weekly grooming sessions should include body checks for lumps (cysts, warts and fatty tumors), hot spots and other skin or coat problems. While harmless skin lumps are common in older dogs, many can be malignant, and your vet should examine any abnormality. Mole-like black patches or growths on any body part require immediate veterinary inspection. Remember, petting and hugging can also turn up little abnormalities.

Be extra-conscious of dry skin, a flaky coat and thinning hair, all signs of possible thyroid disease. Check for fleas and flea dirt (especially on your dog's underside and around the base of the tail) if you think fleas could be present.

CHAPTER 9

EAR CARE

Check your dog's ears weekly…are they clean and fresh-smelling? Have your vet show you the proper way to clean them, never probing into the ear canal. Know the signs of a problem: foul odor, dark discharge, small brown dots that could indicate ear mites. Remember, too, that many old dogs grow deaf with age. Sure, a

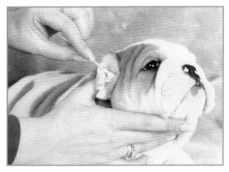

If using a cotton swab for ear cleaning, you must have a gentle, steady hand and a pup who won't fidget. Cotton balls or pads are safer, as they pose less risk of probing into the ear canal.

smart dog develops selective hearing and sometimes will not "hear" you, but you'll know it's a true hearing defect when your Bulldog no longer hears the clinking of the treat jar. Time and experience will show you what changes and allowances to make if your dog develops hearing loss.

EYE CARE

Your Bulldog's vision may deteriorate with age. A bluish haze is common in geriatric dogs and does not impair vision, but you should always check with your vet about any change in the eyes to determine if it's harmless or a problem. As part of your grooming routine, you also will check the areas around the eyes and keep them clean.

THE HIND END

How about his other end? Does your dog chew at his rear or scoot and rub it on the carpet? That's a sign of impacted anal glands. Have your vet express those glands (it's not a job for amateurs). Do annual stool cultures to check for intestinal parasites; hook-, whip- and roundworms can cause weight and appetite loss, poor coat quality and all manner of intestinal problems, which can weaken your dog's resistance to other canine diseases. See your vet if any of those signs appear.

Tapeworms, common parasites that come from fleas, look like grains of rice in the stool.

HEART DISEASE
Heart disease is common in all canines, yet it is one that dog owners most frequently overlook. Symptoms include panting and shortness of breath, chronic coughing, especially at night or upon first waking in the morning, and changes in sleeping habits. Heart disease can be treated if you catch it early, so be alert.

KIDNEY DISEASE
Kidney disease also can be treated successfully if caught early. Dogs seven and up should be tested annually for kidney and liver function. If your dog drinks and urinates too much or has accidents in the house, get to your vet. Kidney disease can be managed with special diets.

HOME CARE OF YOUR BULLDOG

Overview

- The attention you give to your Bulldog's health in between veterinary visits is the best preventive medicine.
- Two of the most important care regimens for your dog are home dental care and keeping him at a healthy weight.
- Grooming and petting your Bulldog can uncover abnormalities that need veterinary attention. Be diligent about regularly checking your dog's skin and coat for lumps, bumps, rashes, hair loss or other signs of problems that might not be readily noticeable.
- Make attention to your dog's eyes, ears and anal sacs part of your grooming routine for overall health.
- Heart and kidney problems can be common in canines but are very treatable; early diagnosis greatly increases the chances of the treatment's being successful.

Feeding Your Bulldog

Few dog issues are more confusing—or more critical—than *food*! Your Bulldog should have a quality food that is appropriate for his age and lifestyle. Only a premium-quality food will provide the proper balance of vitamins, minerals and fatty acids that is necessary to support healthy bones, muscles, skin and coat. The major dog-food manufacturers have developed their formulas with strict quality controls, using only quality ingredients obtained from reliable sources. The labels on the food bags tell you what products are in the food (beef, chicken, corn, etc), and list the ingredients in descending order of

Shallow bowls are best for the Bulldog because of his short muzzle.

weight or amount in the food. Do not add your own supplements, "people food" or extra vitamins to the food. You will only upset the nutritional balance of the food, which could affect growth of your pup or maintenance of your adult Bulldog. If your vet or breeder feels that your Bulldog will benefit from a vitamin supplement of some kind, he will instruct you on how much and what type. Do not start adding supplements on your own.

A healthy diet for the Bulldog is one that contains balanced and complete nutrition for the dog's stage of life and physical condition.

The premium dog-food brands now offer foods for every breed size, age and activity level. As with human infants, puppies require a diet different from that of an adult canine. Growth-formula foods contain protein and fat levels that are appropriate for the different-sized breeds. Your Bulldog has different nutritional requirements from larger breeds like the Golden Retriever, who experience growth spurts, or smaller breeds like the

The breeder must bottle-feed a young puppy when, for whatever reason, the pup will not nurse from his mother.

Yorkshire Terrier. As a rule, puppy-food formulas are designed to promote healthy growth, not rapid growth.

In the world of quality dog foods, there are enough choices to befuddle even experienced dog folks. Don't be intimidated by all those dog-food bags on the store shelves. Read the labels on the bags (how else can you learn what's in those foods?) and do not choose a soybean-based product for your Bulldog. Call the company's information number on the dog-food bag if you want to learn more. Ask your breeder and your vet what food they recommend for your Bulldog pup. A basic knowledge of canine nutrition will provide the tools you need to offer your dog a diet that is best for his long-term health.

Despite all of the choices out there, providing complete nutrition for your puppy will actually be quite easy once you've decided on what type of food to feed. Dog-food companies spend millions of dollars on research to determine what will be a healthy diet for your dog, so you should be confident that your pup's food is providing him with the nutrients that he needs, in the correct amounts. This is why supplementing the food is not only unnecessary but it can even be harmful. Neither too much nor too little of certain nutrients is healthy.

Young puppies are usually fed up to four times a day, with the frequency of feedings reduced as they grow up. Youngsters do well with having their dry food moistened with warm water. You want the puppy to enjoy his food and you want him to look healthy: round but not fat, with a healthy-looking coat. Your breeder should have been feeding the litter a premium puppy food and you should continue on with the same brand, at least initially. If you plan to switch from the food fed by your breeder, take home a small supply of the breeder's food to mix with your own to aid your puppy's adjustment to his new food.

As for amounts to feed, some Bulldog breeders suggest allowing a puppy to eat as much as he wants at mealtimes, as long as he's getting sufficient activity and remaining in fit condition. A chubby puppy will need his food intake limited, but it's important to do so only under the advice of a vet with experience in the breed. A weight-loss diet during the growth period is a tricky thing to do correctly, as the pup needs proper nutrition for healthy development.

While free feeding, which means leaving a bowl of food out at all times so that your dog can eat as he pleases, is not recommended for most breeds, many Bulldog puppies seem to do fine with it. Owners, however, may choose

to stick with a set feeding schedule to aid in house-training and to gauge their dogs' appetites. By the time the Bulldog is six months old,

Most Bulldogs are enthusiastic eaters and will come running at mealtimes.

he can be on a twice-daily feeding schedule; many owners feel that a morning/evening feeding routine is convenient. Many times a dog's feeding schedule is determined by the owner's daily schedule, and that should be fine for the adult Bulldog.

CHAPTER 10

A Bulldog can stay on a puppy-formula dry food until 12 months old, possibly longer. Most Bulldogs are switched to adult food between one year and 18 months of age. Again, changes should be done gradually. If your Bulldog was doing well on a certain brand of puppy food, the easiest change would be to feed the adult formula of the same brand. For a dog that tends to gain weight, "light" adult foods are an option.

The best treats for your Bulldog are dog treats, not table scraps. Keep in mind that certain foods, such as nuts, grapes, raisins, onions and chocolate, are toxic to dogs and can harm their health, causing problems such

as anemia, paralysis, even death. Crunchy dog biscuits have dental benefits, removing plaque as the dog chews; some even help minimize "doggie breath."

Let us emphasize once more that lean is healthy, fat is not. Research has proven that obesity is a major canine killer. Quite simply, a lean dog lives longer than one who is overweight. And that doesn't even reflect the better quality of life for the lean dog that can run, jump and play without the burden of those extra pounds. If your Bulldog needs to lose some weight, formulate a healthy eating and exercise plan for him under the guidance of your vet. Reducing calories should not mean reducing nutrition.

To further complicate the dog-food dilemma, there are proponents of raw-food diets. Some dog owners prefer to feed their dogs a completely natural diet rather than tradi-tional manufactured dog food.

A suitable puppy diet will contain extra protein and fat for the growth period, but should not contain nutrient levels that will promote rapid growth.

The debate on raw and/or all-natural vs. manufactured dog food is a fierce one, with some raw-food proponents claiming that raw diets have cured their dogs' allergies and other chronic ailments. If you are interested in this alternative feeding method, you must know what you are doing before attempting to try it. There are books and websites dedicated to the topic, and you are wise to check with your vet, ask your breeder and talk to people who are experienced in feeding raw-food diets to their dogs.

The bottom line is this: what you feed your Bulldog is a major factor in his overall health and longevity. It's worth your investment in extra time and dollars to provide the best diet for your Bulldog.

FEEDING YOUR BULLDOG

Overview

- Know how to interpret dog-food labels and also take your breeder's and vet's advice regarding the best diet for your Bulldog's life stage and physical condition.
- Puppies need more frequent feedings in smaller amounts. The schedule changes as the dog grows, usually to twice a day, once in the morning and once in the evening.
- Some breeders feel that free feeding is fine for the Bulldog; however, if this does not work and your dog gains/loses weight or becomes finicky about his food, you will have to get him on a regular schedule.
- Suitable treats for your Bulldog are dog treats, not people-food tidbits. People foods can cause stomach upset or worse, as some foods are toxic to dogs.
- If interested in a raw-food diet, do your research! This is not something to jump into without knowing how to provide complete nutrition.

Grooming Your Bulldog

A big plus for owning the Bulldog is that this is basically a "wash and wear" breed, so coat care will be kept to a minimum. Do understand before purchasing your Bulldog, though, that he will need some grooming and special attention to his hygiene, especially keeping the facial wrinkles clean.

It will also be helpful to have a table on which to groom your dog. This can be a regular grooming table with a grooming arm to which you can attach the dog's leash, or you can use a table in your home, adding an eye hook to

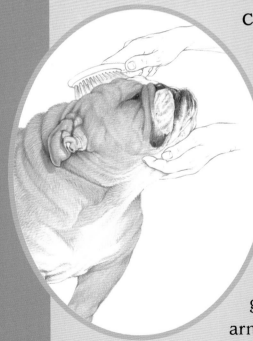

A soft-bristled brush will suffice for going over your Bulldog's short coat.

the ceiling above the table to hold the leash and rubber matting to give a non-slip surface. Although the Bulldog is not a heavily groomed breed, having him standing securely on a table while you brush him, wipe him down and trim his toenails will be more comfortable for both of you.

Brushing your Bulldog with a soft-bristled brush is recommended to keep your dog's coat looking shiny and clean. Brushing removes dead hair and debris in the coat while distributing the coat's natural oils to keep it shiny and healthy. A thorough once-over, a few times weekly, will do the trick. Most Bulldogs enjoy the feeling of being brushed and relish the one-on-one time with their owners. During your Bulldog's shedding times, which occur in the spring and fall, daily brushings will help keep shed hair around the home to a minimum, as the dead hair will be caught in the brush, not left on

Incorporate toothbrushing into your grooming routine. A dog that is acclimated to the process as a puppy will be much easier to deal with as an adult.

You might use a slicker brush during shedding times, as this is more effective in removing dead hair from the coat.

your carpets, clothing and furniture. A grooming mitt that fits over your hand is excellent for the close coat of the Bulldog.

A bath is certainly recommended when your dog is very dirty, but often a rubdown with a damp cloth will be ample for cleaning. Frequent bathing will deprive the dog's coat of important oils. In general, baths are recommended twice a year, in the spring and the fall, unless the need arises at other times, such as a roll in something smelly! Show dogs are bathed more frequently, usually before every show.

You can bathe a Bulldog in your bathtub, in a sink, outdoors in warm weather, wherever you choose, as long as you have a faucet or hose within reach to thoroughly soak and rinse the coat. You will need a mild shampoo, one made for dogs, not for humans. A little mineral oil or eye ointment in each eye and a cotton ball in each ear will keep water from entering these areas.

Thoroughly wet the dog's coat, apply shampoo down the dog's back (not on the head and face) and work it into a lather, getting all of the hard-to-reach places. For the face, use a lathered-up washcloth, making sure to get all of the wrinkles. You can also wipe down both sides of the ear flaps with the washcloth. When you are ready to rinse, do so thoroughly, getting all shampoo out of the coat and wrinkles.

Use heavy towels to dry the dog. You should keep him indoors and away from drafts until he is completely dry. Breeders recommend a bit of petroleum jelly on the Bulldog's nose following a bath to help keep it soft. If you need to dry your Bulldog quickly, a blow dryer on the lowest heat, held at a safe distance, will do the trick.

You will need to clean and maintain the facial wrinkles regularly, not just at bath time. Depending on your Bulldog, you may clean the wrinkles daily or a few times weekly. You can use either a damp washcloth or a washcloth with dog shampoo on it, as you do during the dog's bath. Whichever you choose, always rinse the wrinkles completely and dry them thoroughly. You should also wash the nose and apply petroleum jelly, again as you would after a bath. If your Bulldog has tear stains around the eyes, there are products available from your pet store that will remove them.

It is important to trim your dog's toenails, and it is best to start this within a week of bringing him home. Purchase a quality toenail trimmer for pets. You may want to purchase a styptic stick in case you trim the

nail too short and bleeding starts. If your dog's toenails are light in color, you will easily see the blood vessel (the "quick") that runs inside

the nail. However, the quick is a bit more difficult to see in dark-toed dogs, and you may nick the blood vessel until you are more familiar with trimming the nails. If you do not start trimming the nails at a young age, so that your dog is used to his

Not a water dog by trade, the Bulldog may or may not enjoy bath time! Whether or not he likes being bathed, you at least want his cooperation.

pedicures, you will have greater difficulty accustoming him to the procedure as your Bulldog becomes larger, heavier and more difficult to hold.

Ear cleaning and tooth-brushing are also regular grooming maintenance tasks that are essential to your Bulldog's good health. We've already mentioned the dental products available to dogs and their owners, and you can incorporate tooth-brushing as part of the face-washing routine. Ears should be checked regularly and kept free of wax and debris. Using an ear-cleaning product and a soft cotton wipe, gently clean inside the

The breed standard states that the Bulldog's nails are "short and stubby." You must tend to them regularly to keep their desired short length; leaving them too long can cause the feet to splay, which can result in further problems.

ear, never probing deeper than you can see or probing into the ear canal. Any foul odor, thick discharge or dark specks in the ear should be brought to your vet's attention.

To wrap it up: this is a dog that can be easy to groom if you get into a routine. Brush him regularly, trim his toenails every month or so and wipe him down with a damp cloth in between baths. Watch the folds around his face, eyes and muzzle and clean them on a daily basis, if necessary.

Give him a bath as needed. You will now have a good-looking, fresh-smelling Bulldog with whom you will be proud to be seen!

The Bulldog is not a trimmed breed, although some owners like to clean up the muzzle by trimming the whiskers down.

GROOMING YOUR BULLDOG

Overview

- Your Bulldog's short coat makes his coat-care needs minimal; regular brushing will suffice to remove debris and dead hair from the coat.
- Bathing too frequently will dry out the skin and coat; twice-yearly baths are enough unless your dog gets into something dirty.
- Make it a point to check your Bulldog's wrinkles every day and clean them as often as needed.
- Incorporate your routine "housekeeping" tasks into the grooming routine—toothbrushing, eye care, ear care and nail clipping.

Keeping Your Bulldog Active

Many owners are looking for fun and challenging things to do with their dogs, and there are many activities to keep you and your Bulldog very busy, active and interested. If you've completed a puppy training class, you may want to work toward the AKC's Canine Good Citizen® certificate. This is a program that shows how your dog minds his manners in certain situations, such as with you, with strangers, in public places and with other dogs. This program is available to all dogs (any pure-bred or mixed-breed dog) of

A Bulldog's heavy body construction does not lend itself to his being an Olympic swimmer, but he may enjoy splashing around in the surf under your watchful eye.

all ages, and it's both fun and useful for everyday life. The ten exercises that make up the test are: accepting a friendly stranger, sitting politely for petting, accepting light grooming and examination from a stranger, walking on a loose lead, coming when called, responding calmly to another dog, responding to distractions, down on command and remaining calm when the owner is out of sight for three minutes. Upon successful completion, the dog will receive an AKC Canine Good Citizen® certificate and the CGC suffix for his name.

Obedience is a long-established sport at which Bulldogs can excel. Obedience trials are held either by themselves or in conjunction with an AKC dog show. There are many levels, starting with Novice, whereupon completion of three passing "legs" the dog will earn a Companion Dog (CD) title. The levels then continue in difficulty, with Open at the second level;

A fenced yard or other safe enclosure will certainly be appreciated by your Bulldog so that he can get those little legs moving!

Puppies love chew toys, especially when teething, but pups and adults of all ages usually enjoy occupying themselves with a favorite toy.

the dog earns a Companion Dog Excellent (CDX) title upon completion of three successful legs. The next level is Utility, in which the Utility Dog (UD) title is at stake. The Utility level includes advanced exercises such as off-lead work, silent hand signals and picking the right dumbbells from a group of dumbbells. Not many dogs reach this level, and it is a major accomplishment for both owner and dog when a Utility title is achieved.

The first Bulldog obedience trial was held in northern California in 1970 and had an entry of nine Bulldogs. Since that time, Bulldogs have done well in obedience but, as one Bulldogger told me, her dog did "teach her humility." Training a Bulldog for competitive obedience can certainly be a challenge! Nonetheless, numerous Bulldogs have earned their Utility Dog titles.

Agility is another sport that may be an option for the Bulldog. However, it is a vigorous activity, requiring speed and accuracy as the dog runs, jumps and balances his way through an obstacle course. If your Bulldog has any breathing problems, agility will be too strenuous for him, so use good judgment when deciding whether or not to explore agility with your Bulldog.

Obedience and agility have become so popular with the dog-loving public that you should have little difficulty finding a club or class with a training facility. You will find it a great experience to work with your dog and meet new people with whom you will have a common interest. Training for any competitive dog sport takes time and interest on your part, and a willing dog working on the other end of the leash.

For a less active but equally, if not more so,

rewarding pursuit, your Bulldog will likely make a wonderful therapy dog. There are various organizations that train and certify dogs and their owners for pet therapy work, which consists of taking your dog to places like hospitals, nursing homes, schools and care centers to visit the residents there, bringing companionship, comfort and cuddles.

The easiest way to keep your dog active and fit is to take him for walks every morning and evening. This will be good for you, too! Playing games with your dog will delight him. Chasing a ball or tugging on a knotted sock or rope toy are always great fun for a dog; even better, playing games means that you are participating in activities together! Never give your Bulldog rawhides and never offer toys or balls that are small enough for him to swallow. If he can swallow it, you can bet that he will, and an expensive trip to the veterinarian may follow. Also remember, when playing games, walking and doing any kind of activity with your Bulldog, to not allow him to become overheated.

KEEPING YOUR BULLDOG ACTIVE

Overview

- There are many organized activities in which you and your Bulldog can participate, including Canine Good Citizen® testing, obedience and agility competition, therapy-dog work and more.
- Keeping your Bulldog fit means keeping him active with things like regular walks and play sessions.
- The type of exercise that your Bulldog will enjoy most is anything that you and he can do together!

Your Healthy Bulldog

One of the first things you will do with your new puppy is bring him to the vet. You should have chosen a vet before puppy comes home, someone who knows the Bulldog. It is important to find a vet with experience in the breed and who is knowledgeable about the care of and potential problems seen in the breed. Your breeder may be able to recommend someone in your area. Sometime during puppy's first week home, bring him to the vet for an overall checkup. On your first visit, take along the pup's health

Your veterinarian will manage your Bulldog's vaccination and booster schedule throughout the dog's life.

records that you got from your breeder. This will have a record of the puppy's shots thus far so that the veterinarian will know which series of shots your pup should be getting. You should also take in a fecal sample for a worm test.

A healthy dog starts out as a healthy puppy produced by careful breeding.

It is helpful if the vet is located within ten miles of your home, not just for convenience's sake but also in case there is an emergency and your Bulldog needs to see the vet quickly. Find a veterinarian that you like and trust. Be confident that he knows what he is doing and see that the office looks and smells clean. It is your right to check on fees before setting up an appointment. Many veterinary clinics have several vets practicing there, so try and see the same vet at each visit, as he will personally know the history of your dog and your dog will be familiar with him. Inquire if the clinic takes emergency calls and, if they do not,

Bulldogs enjoy time outdoors, but owners must use caution in hot weather, as the breed is prone to heat-related problems. On hot and humid days, a Bulldog would do best indoors in an air-conditioned house.

as many no longer do, get the name, address and telephone number of the emergency veterinary service in your area and keep this handy with your vet's phone number.

Your Bulldog puppy will visit the vet every few weeks for his vaccinations. As an adult, your Bulldog will need booster shots, the frequency of which will vary. Regardless of vaccine frequency, every adult Bulldog should visit his veterinarian once a year for a full checkup, including an annual heartworm test before he can receive another year of heartworm preventive. Most importantly, the annual visit keeps your vet apprised of your pet's health progress, and the hands-on exam often turns up problems and small abnormalities that the owner can't see or feel. As he reaches his senior years, around the age of seven, your Bulldog should start to visit the vet twice yearly, as the healthcare protocol for seniors is more

extensive. Plus, more frequent visits allow the vet to catch health problems as early as possible, which can make a big difference in the success of the treatment and cure.

VACCINATIONS
One of the first things your vet will do is set up a schedule for your pup's remaining vaccinations. Vaccine protocol for puppies varies with many veterinarians, but most recommend a series of three "combination" shots given at three- to four-week intervals. Your puppy should have had his first shot before he left his breeder. Combination shots vary, and a single injection may contain five, six, seven, or even eight vaccines in one shot. Many breeders and veterinarians feel the potency in high-combination vaccines can negatively compromise a puppy's immature immune system, so they recommend fewer vaccines in one shot or even separating vaccines into

individual injections. The wisest and most conservative course is to administer only one shot during a vet exam rather than two or three shots at the same time. That means additional visits to your veterinarian with your puppy and adult dog, but your Bulldog's healthy immune system is worth those extra trips.

The vaccines recommended by the American Veterinary Medical Association (AVMA) are called core vaccines, those which protect against diseases most dangerous to your puppy and adult dog. These include distemper (canine distemper virus, CDV), fatal in puppies; canine parvovirus (CPV or parvo), highly contagious and also fatal in puppies and at-risk dogs; canine adenovirus (CAV-2), highly contagious and high risk for pups under 16 weeks of age; and canine hepatitis (CAV-1) highly contagious, pups at high risk. These are generally combined into

one injection. Rabies immunization is required by law in all 50 states, with the vaccine given three weeks after the complete series of the puppy shots.

Non-core vaccines no longer routinely recommended by the AVMA, except when the risk is present, are canine

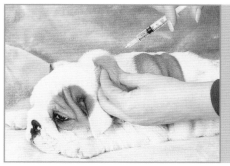

To minimize the number of necessary injections, the essential inoculations are often combined into a single shot.

parainfluenza, leptospirosis, canine coronavirus, *Bordetella* (canine cough) and Lyme (borreliosis). Your veterinarian will alert you if there is a risk of these non-fatal diseases in your town or neighborhood so you can immunize accordingly.

BREED-SPECIFIC CONCERNS
The Bulldog is a brachy-cephalic breed of dog. Other

similar breeds include the French Bulldog, Boxer, Boston Terrier and any breed that has a "flat face." Because of this facial structure and "pushed-in" nose, all of these breeds can have difficulty breathing, especially during hot weather. Care must be taken not to let your Bulldog become over-heated in the summer. Do not take your dog out for a run on a hot day, and do not leave him out in the yard in the sun. Exercise is important for a Bulldog to build stamina and prevent obesity, but don't overdo it, particularly when it is hot or humid. Always have shade and fresh cold water available for him. You must also watch out for your Bulldog's breathing in stressful situations.

There are some health problems to which the Bulldog is prone. Every new owner should be aware of these problems and how to recognize them in case they occur:

Elongated soft palate and other breathing problems: Because of the breed's flat face, Bulldogs can be affected with elongated palates, which can cause respiratory failure after strenuous exercise. It can also cause snoring and noisy breathing. Surgery can alleviate this problem by restructuring the soft palate. Stenotic nares (pinched nostrils) and small trachea are other problems that can be seen in the Bulldog and contribute to breathing problems.

Entropion and ectropion: Both of these conditions are eyelid abnormalities. Entropion is when the lid turns inward, causing the eyelashes to rub against the cornea. This results in discomfort and injury to the cornea. Entropion is considered to be an inherited problem in some breeds, including the Bulldog, and you should make certain that the breeder has had the sire and dam checked for this problem. Ectropion is the opposite of entropion. In ectroption, the eyelid, usually the lower lid, turns outward. Both conditions call for corrective surgery.

Muzzle pyoderma and wrinkle dermatitis: Because the Bulldog is heavily wrinkled, pustules can develop on the pigmented part of the muzzle. In addition, dermatitis can be found in the facial and nasal folds as well as under the tail. Clean the folds well, as often as needed, as part of your grooming routine, and if the problem does develop, see your veterinarian for antibiotics to clear it up.

Hip dysplasia: This is a major concern, as it is in many medium-sized and large breeds. Hip dysplasia is an inherited disease in which the head of the femur (thigh bone) fails to fit into the socket in the hip bone and there is not enough muscle mass to hold the joint together. This can often be a very painful

problem for the dog, causing him to limp or to move about with great difficulty. There are therapeutic, medical and surgical treatments that have proven to be successful, but affected dogs should not be bred. All Bulldogs that are bred should have normal hips as determined by an x-ray and

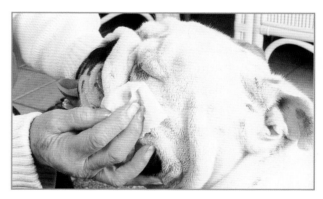

certified by the Orthopedic Foundation for Animals (OFA).

HEARTWORM AND OTHER INTERNAL PARASITES

Heartworms are parasites that propagate inside your dog's heart and will ultimately kill him if left untreated. Now found in all 50 states, heartworm is delivered

Perhaps the most important grooming task for Bulldog owners is keeping those facial wrinkles clean! Left unattended, moisture and bacteria can build up in the folds, causing odor and even infection.

CHAPTER 13

through a mosquito bite. Even indoor dogs should take heartworm preventive, which can be given daily or monthly in pill form, or in a shot given every six months. Most of the pills come in tasty flavors so that your dog thinks he's getting a treat instead of medication. Heartworm preventives require a prescription from your veterinarian. A heartworm test is required before the vet will dispense the medication.

Roundworms, tapeworms, hookworms, threadworms and whipworms are internal parasites that can cause a host of problems in dogs. Most worms are evident in a dog's stool, which is why your dog's stool sample is tested by the vet. Puppies are dewormed as a matter of course, and adults that are found to have internal parasites are prescribed an appropriate dewormer. Most heartworm preventives protect dogs against other internal parasites as well.

FLEAS AND TICKS

Fleas have been around for millennia, and it's likely that you will wage flea battle sometime during your Bulldog's lifetime. Fortunately, today there are several low-toxic, effective flea weapons to aid you in your flea war.

Tick-borne diseases such as Lyme disease (borreliosis), ehrlichiosis and Rocky Mountain spotted fever are now found in almost every state and can affect humans as well as dogs. Dogs that live in or visit areas where ticks are present, whether seasonally or year-round, should be protected.

Modern science has yielded a number of very effective tick and flea drugs. Some of the most effective preventives are: imidacloporid, a spot-on treatment applied between the shoulder blades that will kill adult fleas for 30 days; lufenuron, an insect-growth regulator given as a monthly pill that prevents flea eggs from hatching; fipronil, also a spot-on treatment that will kill fleas for 90 days and ticks for up to 30 days; and selamectin, a monthly spot-on that protects against heartworm, fleas, ticks and certain mites.

Your veterinarian can advise you which of the current products would be safest and most effective for your Bulldog. Over-the-counter

An important outdoor issue is checking the Bulldog's skin and coat for any sign of parasites, debris in the coat or skin allergens.

flea and tick collars offer only limited protection and are risky at best. You want to use a product that you know is effective to prevent your dog from experiencing flea- and tick-related health problems. Homespun remedies include brewer's yeast, garlic, citronella and other herbal products, but none have been scientifically proven to be effective.

SPAYING/NEUTERING

Should you or shouldn't you? This is almost a non-question, since spaying or neutering is the best health-insurance policy that you can give your Bulldog. Statistics prove that females spayed before their first heat cycle (estrus) have 90% less of a risk of several common female cancers and other serious female health problems. Males neutered

Happy Bulldogs are those whose owners take precautions so that they can enjoy the great outdoors safely.

before their male hormones kick in, usually before six months of age, enjoy zero to greatly reduced risk of testicular and prostate cancer and other related tumors and infections. Additionally, males will be less likely to roam or become aggressive or display those overt male behaviors that owners find difficult to handle.

Altering your pet Bulldog will not automatically make him fat and lazy, and one need only adjust the dog's diet and increase his exercise if weight gain does occur. Statistically, you will make a positive contribution to the pet overpopulation problem and to your dog's long-term health.

YOUR HEALTHY BULLDOG

Overview

- Find a vet who knows Bulldogs, with whom you are comfortable, who offers the services you need and who is conveniently located.
- Yearly checkups are the minimum for an adult in good health. Once your Bulldog reaches his senior years, around age seven, he should see the vet twice yearly so that any problems can be detected as early as possible.
- Discuss your dog's vaccinations with your vet so that you agree on a safe course of inoculation for your Bulldog.
- Familiarize yourself with the hereditary conditions that can occur in the Bulldog. The breeder should have done all of the available testing, but tests do not exist for every condition.
- Learn how to protect your Bulldog from internal and external parasites.
- Spaying and neutering offer important benefits to your individual dog and the canine population at large.

The Aging Bulldog

As your Bulldog starts aging, he will start to slow down. He will not play as hard or as long as he used to, and he will sleep more. He will find the sunbeam in the morning hours and take a long nap. At this time, you will probably put him on a senior-formula dog food and will watch his weight even more carefully than you have been, as it is more important than ever not to let your senior citizen become obese. You will notice that his muzzle will become gray, and you may see opacities in his eyes, signs of cataracts.

Bulldogs remain loyal and alert companions in their senior years.

As he becomes older, he may even become arthritic. Continue your walks, making them shorter, and give him a baby aspirin (but do not use any other type of pain reliever for humans) when he appears to be stiff. Keep up with his grooming, as both you and your Bulldog will like to have him looking and smelling his best. Watch for lumps and bumps, and have any that you discover checked by the veterinarian. Hopefully they are harmless, but you want to be sure that they are not symptoms of a serious problem. Incontinence can also become a problem with the older dog. This is frustrating for you and can be hard on the carpets, but your Bulldog hasn't become "unhousebroken"; rather, his excretory muscle control is fading.

Your senior Bulldog will still be an active part of your life, albeit at a slower pace, so be sure to give him all the same love and affection, with some special attention in his golden years.

The Bulldog has an average lifespan of around ten years and, with good care, your dog's life can be extended longer than expected.

Your senior Bulldog will certainly make the most of his retirement years, relaxing in style!

Veterinary care has changed much over the last decade or two, as has medical care for humans. Your veterinarian can now do much to prolong your dog's life if you want to spend the money. While this will extend your dog's life, it will not bring back his youth. Your primary concern should be to help your pet live out his life comfortably; there are medications that can be helpful for this goal. Whatever, try to put your dog, and his well-being and comfort, ahead of your emotions and do what will be best for your Bulldog.

When the time comes and your Bulldog has reached the end of his life, always cherish the memories of the many wonderful years that he gave to you and your family. With that thought, it may not be long before you are looking for a new Bulldog puppy for the household. And there you are, back at the beginning with a cute bundle of joy, ready for another ten years or more of happiness!

THE AGING BULLDOG

Overview

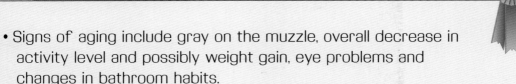

- Signs of aging include gray on the muzzle, overall decrease in activity level and possibly weight gain, eye problems and changes in bathroom habits.
- The Bulldog's average lifespan is around ten years, but the breed can definitely live longer with proper healthcare.
- Your job as the owner of a senior dog is to provide him with the best veterinary care, make his life as comfortable as possible and let him live out his senior years with lots of love and companionship.